金髮姑娘和三隻熊

Goldilocks and the Three Bears

retold by Kate Clynes
illustrated by Louise Daykin

Chinese translation by Sylvia Denham

金髮姑娘正在開開心心地摘花給媽媽，
她走得越來越近森林深處。

金髮姑娘，快停啊，返回家去，
你獨自一人走進森林實在不安全的啊。

Goldilocks was having fun, collecting flowers for her mum.
She was heading deeper and deeper into the woods.

Stop Goldilocks, go back home,
Woods aren't safe when you're all alone.

她找到一間有一個美麗的花園的村屋。
「我要摘那些花，」金髮姑娘說道，「讓我看看有沒有人在家。」

She found a cottage with a beautiful garden.
"I want to pick those flowers," said Goldilocks. "I'll see if anyone's home."

金髮姑娘快停啊，你再敲多一次，
門後面可能有可惡的東西啊。

Stop Goldilocks, knock once more,
There may be something grizzly behind the door.

「喂！」她叫道，
「有沒有人在家呀？」
但那裏什麼回應也沒有。

"Hello!" she called,
"is anybody home?"
But there was no reply.

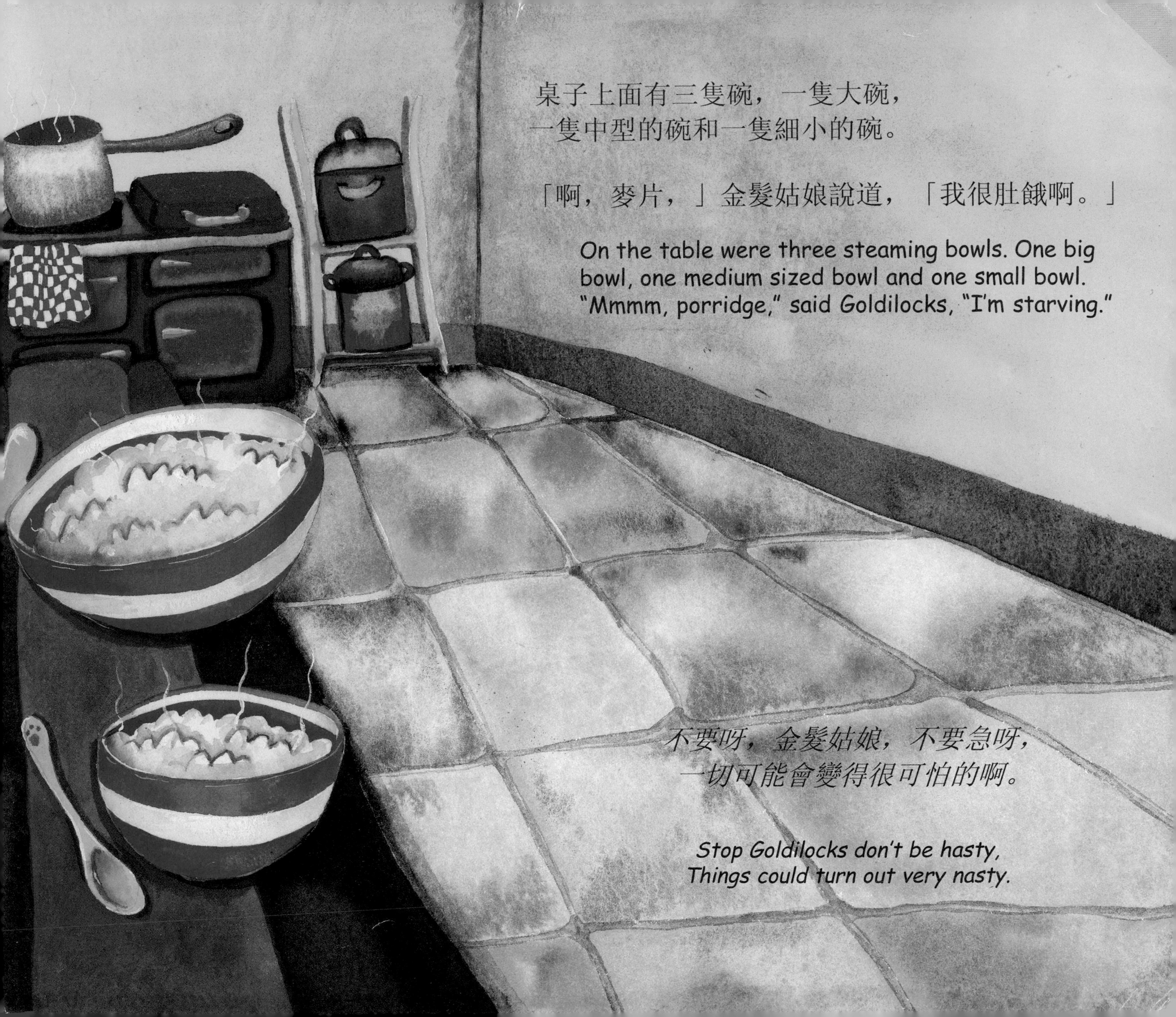

桌子上面有三隻碗，一隻大碗，
一隻中型的碗和一隻細小的碗。

「啊，麥片，」金髮姑娘說道，「我很肚餓啊。」

On the table were three steaming bowls. One big bowl, one medium sized bowl and one small bowl.
"Mmmm, porridge," said Goldilocks, "I'm starving."

不要呀，金髮姑娘，不要急呀，
一切可能會變得很可怕的啊。

Stop Goldilocks don't be hasty,
Things could turn out very nasty.

金髮姑娘從大碗中吃了一大匙，
「哎 唷！」她叫道，麥片太熱了。

Goldilocks took a spoonful from the big bowl.
"Ouch!" she cried. It was far too hot.

她接著走去試中型碗的麥片，
「噢！」麥片太冷了。

Then she tried the middle bowl.
"Yuk!" It was far too cold.

但是那細小的碗的麥片就剛剛好，
金髮姑娘把它全部都吃了！

The small bowl however was just right
and Goldilocks ate the lot!

吃飽了肚子後，金髮姑娘便走到
另一個房間去。

With a nice full tummy, she wandered
into the next room.

等一等呀，金髮姑娘，你不能隨處走，
到處窺探別人的家啊。

Hang on Goldilocks, you can't just roam,
And snoop around someone else's home.

溫暖的壁爐燃點著，壁爐的前面
有三張椅子，一張大椅子，
一張中型的椅子和一張細小的椅子。

In front of the warm, glowing
fire were three chairs.
One big chair, one medium
sized chair and one small chair.

Not Again
Red Riding
Hood

金髮姑娘先爬到大椅子上，但它實在太硬了，
她接著爬到中型的椅子上去，但它實在太柔軟了，
可是細小的椅子卻剛剛適合，
金髮姑娘於是向後靠，突然…

First Goldilocks climbed onto the big chair, but it was just too hard.
Then she climbed onto the medium sized chair,
but it was just too soft.
The little chair, however, felt just right.
Goldilocks was leaning back, when...

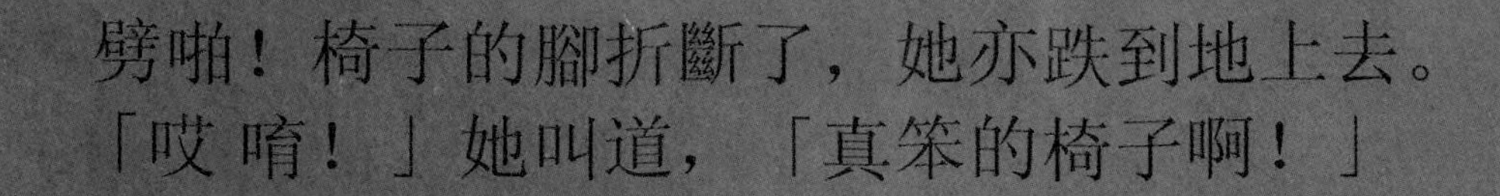

劈啪！椅子的腳折斷了，她亦跌到地上去。
「哎 唷！」她叫道，「真笨的椅子啊！」

哎呀，金髮姑娘，你怎麼搞的啊？
快起來，起來，快快走啊。

SNAP! The legs broke
and she fell onto the floor.
"Ouch," she cried.
"Stupid chair!"

Oh no Goldilocks, what have you done?
Get up quick, get up and run.

金髮姑娘覺得很疲倦，
於是便走上樓上。
在睡 房中有三張床，
一張大床，一張中型的床和
一張細小的床。

Goldilocks felt tired so she made her way upstairs.
In the bedroom were three beds.
One big bed, one medium sized bed and one small bed.

她爬上大床，但是它實在起伏不平的，
她接著爬上中型的床，但是它的彈力實在太大了，
可是那細小的床就剛剛好，她很快便睡著了。

She climbed up onto the big bed but it was too lumpy. Then she tried the medium sized bed, which was too springy. The small bed however, felt just right and soon she was fast asleep.

起來呀，金髮姑娘，睜開你的眼睛，
你可能會有很大的驚訝啊！

Wake up Goldilocks, open your eyes,
You could be in for a BIG surprise!

就在這時，
三隻熊回到家來，
熊爸爸踢到花籃
摔了一交後，便看到桌子。

Just then the three bears came home.
After tripping over a basket,
Father Bear noticed the table.

「有人吃過我的麥片，」
他用他那粗暴的聲音説道，
「有人吃過我的麥片，」
熊媽媽以她的中等聲音回應道，

"Someone's been eating my porridge," he said in a loud gruff voice.
"Someone's been eating my porridge," echoed Mother Bear in a medium voice.

「有人吃過我的麥片，」小熊用他細小的聲音說道，「還吃過清光呢！」。

"Someone's been eating my porridge," cried Baby Bear in a small voice, "and they've eaten it all up!"

三隻飢餓的熊變得有點兒緊張，
可是一個採花的怪物也不
致於太可怕吧。

Three very hungry bears, feeling slightly wary,
But a flower-collecting monster
doesn't sound too scary.

他們手拉著手，走進客廳，
「有人坐過我的椅子，」熊爸爸用他那粗暴的聲音說道，
「有人坐過我的椅子，」熊媽媽以她的中等聲音回應道，

Holding hands, they crept into the living room.
"Someone's been sitting in my chair,"
said Father Bear in a loud gruff voice.
"Someone's been sitting in my chair,"
echoed Mother Bear in a medium voice.

「有人坐過我的椅子，」小熊用他細小的聲音叫道，
「你們看，他們還把椅子毀壞了！」
他哇地一聲哭起來。

"Someone's been sitting in my chair," cried Baby Bear
in a small voice, "and look, they've broken it!"
He burst into tears.

他們現在很憂慮，
於是靜悄悄地走上
樓梯到睡房去。

Now they were very worried.
Quietly they tiptoed up the
stairs into the bedroom.

三隻焦慮的熊
不知道會發現什麼，
可能是一隻既兇惡，
而又會弄壞椅子的怪物呢。

Three grizzly bears, unsure
of what they'll find,
Some chair-breaking monster
of the meanest kind.

「有人睡過我的床，」熊爸爸用他那粗暴的聲音說道，

"Someone's been sleeping in my bed," said Father Bear in a loud gruff voice.

「有人睡過我的床，」熊媽媽以她的中等聲音回應道，

"Someone's been sleeping in my bed," echoed Mother Bear in a medium voice.

「有人睡過我的床，」
小熊用絕不細小的聲音哭叫道，
「你們看！」

"Someone's been sleeping in my bed," wailed
Baby Bear in a far from small voice,
"and look!"

他的聲音弄醒了
金髮姑娘，
她大聲尖叫。

The noise woke
Goldilocks up and she
screamed.

當三隻熊逐漸
不再驚訝時…

While the bears were
recovering from their shock...

金髮姑娘跳下床，跑下樓梯，
抓住空的花籃逃跑了。

Goldilocks leapt out of bed, ran down the stairs,
grabbed her empty basket and fled.

金髮姑娘，你真活該，
那些熊嚇你一頓，
但你要知道啊，
那三隻熊也是同樣的驚慌呢！

Well Goldilocks, it serves you right,
Those bears gave you a terrible fright.
But here's a secret that must be shared,
The three poor bears were just as scared!